Pray. Praise. Slay. Repeat.

Finding Joy and Peace in the Midst of Life's Storms

Shae Sterling

Unless otherwise noted, scripture quotations are taken from The Holy Bible, New International Version. Grand Rapids: Zondervan House, 1984. Print.

Laurel Publishing House

Ordering Information: Quantity sales- Special discounts are available on quantity purchases by corporations, associations, religious organizations, and other charities. For more details, contact publisher at info@LPHbooks.com.

Printed in the United States of America
Published simultaneously in Canada

November 2018 First Edition
18 17 16 15 14 13/10 9 8 7 6 5 4 3 2 1

You may not understand every detail of the plan or how it is going to come together, but trust God and step out on faith. You will be amazed at the results!

"For I know the plans I have for you declares the Lord, plans to prosper you and not to harm you, plans to give you hope and a future." Jeremiah 29:11

DEDICATION

Aunt Carol,
You taught me how to be strong in the face of adversity,
and you showed me what it truly means to never give up.
You are the embodiment of courage and love. I miss our
daily conversations. I miss your humor, your delicious
cooking, your infectious laughter, and your bright smile.
You were more than my aunt; you were my best friend.
Until we meet again, I love you Boo!

Carol Adriane Sterling

Forever in our hearts

THANK YOU!

Lord, all that I am and hope to be is because you are so wonderful and amazing to me. Thank you for loving me in spite of me. #ForeverGrateful

To the email that started it all: "Have you ever thought about a part time job as a journalist? You really should consider it! God has gifted you with amazing talents. You were intended for greatness and not in a small way." Thank you for encouraging and supporting me through it all, and thanks for believing in me and seeing things that I couldn't see. I love you always.

To my beautiful reason why. Your love inspires and encourages me each day. You challenge me to do better and be better. Your smile brightens up my world, and I am beyond thankful for you. These are some of the many reasons #WhyILoveYou. Forever and a while, in my heart is where you'll stay.

Don't let the problems of today distract you from your
purpose or your promise. Stay focused and keep the
FAITH. Victory is closer thank you think!
~Shae Sterling

INTRODUCTION

January first arrived and was promising to be one of the happiest years of my life. I had an amazing family, great friends, a rewarding career, good health, a strong relationship with God, and a budding romance. Everything seemed to be falling in place, and I smiled thinking "could life get any better?" I would soon discover the answer to that question was one I was not prepared for.

Less than a month after my joyous declaration, what was once bliss quickly turned into distress as I feared losing one of the most important people in my life. My Aunt Carol, so strong and full of life, was now engaged in a full fledge battle FOR her life against a formidable opponent, breast cancer. She had been doing a phenomenal job fighting this battle since 2013; however, her opponent became more aggressive in its approach. It was no longer seeking to steal things like strength, joy, self-confidence, or hope. This time it was fighting with vengeance, aiming to take the very thing that we all treasure, life.

Despite its aggressive nature, we all were confident that Aunt Carol would be victorious. We prayed, believed, and proclaimed her healing. Despite our efforts and Aunt Carol's fearlessness in the face of her foe, on February 12, 2016, the battle was over.

My best friend was gone, and I was absolutely devastated. In that instant dark clouds began to fill the sky, winds began to blow, lightening flashed, thunder rolled, rain poured down from the heavens, and I found myself engulfed by a terrible storm. This storm would rage on for months and months as things in my life seemed to go from bad to worse. Over the course of the next year, the image that was so perfect in January would slowly shatter before my eyes. What was I to do? How could I go on? How would I go on?

Life was hitting me hard all at once, and joy was a word that no longer had any meaning. After all, how could I have joy when my world was falling apart? How could I have joy when my heart was torn to pieces? How could I have joy when I was stuck in the valley with what appeared to be no way out? How could I have joy when all I wanted to do was cry?

God answered those questions in a way I least expected. The key to restoring my joy was not found in a book, people, places, or material things. Ultimately, I discovered joy through a four-word concept pray...praise...slay...repeat. Those four words not only helped me find joy and peace, but they changed my outlook on trials and forever changed my life.

If you have ever found yourself asking similar questions, then I want you to know there is hope. REPEAT AFTER ME: THERE IS HOPE!

Journey with me over the next twenty-one days as I share how God can slay your giants, calm the raging storms of life, fill you with the peace that surpasses all understanding, and give you joy unspeakable.

All you have to do is PRAY, PRAISE, SLAY, REPEAT, and watch God work. The road may not be easy, but God has promised to be with you every step of the way. Are you ready? Let's Go!

DAY 1
"IF GOD LOVES ME,
WHY DID THIS HAPPEN?"

Day after day, that is a question I found myself asking repeatedly. The more I asked, the deeper I found myself reeling in despair. I prayed, trusted, and believed, so why did God not answer my prayer? Why did God break my heart and leave me feeling so angry, disappointed, and hurt?

Months passed, yet it seemed I was no closer to receiving an answer than when I first began asking. Frustration had become my new best friend, and one day I sat down teary eyed, whipped out my phone, and utilized it for something other than texting or communicating on social media. I opened my Bible app and read the verse of the day which came from Psalm 147:3. This really hit home because I was a broken person with a broken heart. I had been wounded and hurt for so long, and joy was nowhere in sight, yet right in front of me was a PROMISE from God saying that HE would heal my broken heart. How could God heal my heart when He was the one who broke it? Instead of allowing these thoughts to spin around in my head, I began to direct my questions to God. I began to communicate my hurt, confusion, and disappointment about what had taken place. When I opened the lines of communication and began to PRAY, I experienced something that had been evading me for quite some time. For the first time in so long, I felt an unexplainable PEACE.

If you are experiencing hurt today and wondering how God could break your heart, I want to share with you what I discovered: SITUATIONS may break our heart, but God does not. On the contrary, He is the one who is there picking up all the broken pieces and putting them back together. It is God who is there in the midnight hours comforting us when all we can do is cry. It is God who is there providing us with strength and encouragement when we feel that we cannot go on.

When you are feeling crushed in spirit, pray and remember these things:

1) **God loves you and is with you even in your valley moments**. Psalm 34:18 says "The Lord is close to the brokenhearted. He rescues those whose spirits are crushed."

2) **God can take the pieces of your heart and put them back together again.** Psalm 147:3 says "He heals the brokenhearted and binds up their wounds."

God is able to heal your wounds, remove the things that hurt you, and make you feel whole again, but you must be willing to give him the broken pieces. Holding on to those feelings of hurt and disappointment not only rob us of joy and peace, but it leaves us empty, broken, and bitter. These feelings overwhelm us in the present and can destroy our future. You see, the enemy does not want us to get past these situations. He wants us to become stuck wallowing in pity, regret, and sorrow. He wants us to be frustrated. He wants us to question God. He wants our minds to be spinning and spinning with negative emotions. He wants us to be so confused and so consumed with anger and anguish that we give up on God and life itself.

God has not called us to live a life of despair. Yes, situations occur that leave us feeling hurt, but God has promised to "turn our mourning into dancing". You must know that this too shall pass, and God can take your pain and give you a praise. It all starts with your willingness to give Him the pieces of your heart.

Dear God,
My plan for this situation was different than your plan, and today I am feeling broken, hurt, and confused. I give you all the pieces of my heart and TRUST you to mend it. Restore my joy and fill me with peace as I stand on your word. Amen.

DAY 2
FOCUS ON THE HEALER
NOT THE HURT

When going through difficult situations, especially loss, I find that many people will ask one question that bothers me a great deal, "How are you?". Inside I sarcastically think "they REALLY don't know how I feel? I just lost my best friend. How should I feel?" However, I know they mean well, so I end up giving the expected response of "fine". Besides, after a few weeks the phone calls, questions, and visits will dwindle, and life will go back to normal for all those around.

To those on the outside looking in, surely I appeared to be doing just fine. By all appearances, I was happy, loving life, and living out the motto "carpe diem". It was rare for one to check social media and not catch a glimpse of me at dinner with friends, relaxing on vacation, being serenaded at concerts, sight-seeing, or trying new things. I was always on the go "living" life or so it seemed.

The truth is that I wanted to stay so busy to elude the reality that came with being still. In my stillness all the laughter and fun faded away, and the sadness flooded in like waves crashing against the shore. In my stillness, I had to face the realization that I was smiling for the camera but dying behind the scenes. In my stillness the hurt and pain became my focus and could no longer be avoided.

I am sure that many of you can relate. I see so many people daily who are walking around hurting yet putting on a façade until they are behind closed doors. It is in those moments of solitude that they begin to wrestle with their situation and focus on the hurt it brings. The problem is that when we focus on the hurt, we are left in a state of brokenness. When we focus on the hurt, we allow ourselves to be fixated on the problem and blinded to the solution. When we focus on the hurt, we open our minds to the size of the struggle instead of the greatness of our God.

Today I encourage you to shift your focus. Focus on the Rock instead of the rockiness. Focus on Problem Solver instead of the problem. Focus on the Master instead of the mess. Focus on the Healer instead of the hurt. When you focus on God and seek his face, you will notice that things begin to change. As you seek Him, he will give you peace. As you seek Him, he will give you joy. As you seek Him, he will give you strength. As you seek him, he will provide all you need to endure the valley and make it to the mountaintop.

Stand strong knowing that God has not forgotten or forsaken you. The word tells us that "weeping may endure for a night, but joy comes in the morning." Today I want you to know that you have endured or may be enduring, but your morning is coming.

I challenge you to look in the mirror and repeat these words: THERE WILL BE JOY AFTER THIS! In spite of what it looks like or what it feels like, THERE WILL BE JOY AFTER THIS!

One thing that I have learned through this experience is that being still is not the horrible thing that I once thought it was. In fact, my stillness gives me the opportunity to focus on God and God alone. My stillness gives me the opportunity to open my heart to Him and find comfort in his arms and strength in his love. It is in my stillness that God turns my heartache into hope.

"The Lord is my shepherd;
I have all that I need.
He lets me rest in the green meadows;
He leads me beside peaceful streams.
He renews my strength.
He guides me along right paths;
Bringing honor to his name.
Even when I walk
Through the darkest valley,
I will not be afraid,
For you are close beside me."
~Psalm 23~

Dear God,

During my storm, help me to focus on you. Help me to seek your face knowing that you are my source of strength, peace, and comfort. Let me not be afraid of still moments but instead help me to be still and know that you are God. Amen.

DAY 3
TRUSTING GOD IN YOUR HURT

I had just finished celebrating my 36th birthday in the Big Apple. It was around 10:00pm, and my mind was still captivated by the production of Phantom of the Opera that I had witnessed moments before. Walking down the melodious street, I could still hear the songs and the words spoken by cast. The cool, crisp air caressing my cheek was a gentle reminder that fall was making its way on the scene. I must admit that my heart has always loved the newness that comes with the change of the seasons, yet I was not prepared for the change that was about to occur in my life.

Early one Saturday morning in October, I opened my eyes, thankful to see another day, and prepared to get up and get moving. Moving was my coping mechanism, but on this day, it proved to be an extremely difficult task. As I attempted to get up, pain gripped my body and forced me back in bed. Over the next few days, my bed and blanket became very familiar to me as leaving seemed nearly impossible without enduring excruciating pain. While in bed, all too familiar thoughts and questions began to swirl around in the blender of my mind as though forming their own smoothie of fear. "Here I am nowhere close to overcoming the grief that has filled my life since losing my aunt, and now something is going on with my health." This couldn't be happening, right? There was no way that God would allow me to experience physical pain on top of the emotional hurt I was already enduring, right? How was I supposed to conquer one if I was suddenly afflicted with the other?

Have you been experiencing health difficulties? Has a loved one gotten sick or passed away? Have you been facing financial problems? Have you lost a job? Have you found yourself wondering what to do and how you would move forward? Have you found yourself in a place where you are filled with hurt? If you've been in that place or if you are currently in that place, I encourage you to TRUST God.

"How can I trust God when I am hurting?" I have asked that question repeatedly, and I am sure many of you have as well. Trusting God in our hurt is not always an easy thing to do, but it is very necessary. I am reminded of a man named Job who endured pain that most of us cannot fathom. He lost his family, his home, his friends, and his livelihood. If that wasn't enough, he was afflicted with a disease that caused the flesh to fall from his bones! While many others would have been consumed by their pain, Job continued to trust God and made one of the most powerful declarations I have ever heard saying, "Though he slay me, yet will I trust him." Glory to

God! Though he slay me, yet will I trust him! Job knew that even in this low point God was still faithful, and it was only God that was going to deliver him. Therefore, Job put his hope and trust in the Lord of Lords.

Often times, we fall into the trap of believing that as followers of Christ life is going to be sunshine and rainbows, and we will never encounter trials. Thus, when we face difficulties, we get discouraged and find it difficult to trust God. The reality is that God never promised that we wouldn't endure, but he did say that He would be with us always. God also promised to supply us with peace that surpasses all understanding to guard our hearts and minds; therefore, in those trying times we can find comfort if we learn stand on God's promises.

Dear God,
Today many things are going on in my life, and I don't know what to do or which way to go. Lord help me to put my trust in you, knowing that you love me, care for me, and will see me through. Amen.

"Trust in the Lord with all your heart and lean not to your own understanding. In all your ways acknowledge him, and He will direct your path." Proverbs 3:5-6

DAY 4
BECAUSE HE LIVES

As long as I can remember, Christmas has been one of my favorite holidays because it is a time of celebration, family, excitement, and reflection. As a child, I remember not being able to sleep the night before because I couldn't wait for Christmas morning. Surprisingly, it was not the presents that kept me awake, but instead it was the anticipation of all my family being in one place making beautiful memories.

This year the memory would be different as it would be the first without the familiar smiling face our beloved Aunt Carol. For the first time in 36 years, I found myself dreading the arrival of Christmas as it only intensified the hurt I was feeling.

At 7:00am I opened my eyes and felt the chill of a cold winter morning. All was quiet in the house, so I ventured into the living room and gazed at the beautiful tree adorned with bright lights and a mixture of ornaments. Christmas had finally arrived, and my heart fluttered with excitement as I saw my daughter's eyes light up with joy. Trinity was only 8, but she reflected the Christmas spirit that my grandmother instilled in each of us.

A few hours later, my family started to pour into the house for breakfast. Afterwards, we would all chat, exchange gifts, and prepare Christmas dinner. The house was full and yet to me seemed so empty. Although I was surrounded by people and laughter, I felt an intense feeling of loneliness and sadness. The feeling of loss was too difficult to bear. I ran out of the house, jumped in my car, drove to the beach, and cried as I watched the sunset on Sunset.

Later that night, I received a surprising call from my cousin who I thought would be having a difficult time since this was the first Christmas without his mom. This call was a great reminder that God knows what we need and exactly when we need it. I was at my lowest and truly felt like giving up, and God used the person I least expected to deliver an encouraging word that placed me on the road to healing. It was a word that gave me hope that I would in fact make it through what seemed to be the most horrific experience of my life. The word was this:

Because He lives, not only can I face tomorrow, but I can get through today.

For those of you that are in the midst of life's storms, and you feel like you just want to give up, I want you to know that because HE lives, not only can you face tomorrow, but you can get through today. You may wonder, "How can I get through this?" The Bible says, "I can do all things through Christ that strengthens me." Therefore, if you and I can DO

ALL things through Christ, then we can GET THROUGH ALL things with Christ!

There will be days where we feel discouraged. There will be days where we are disappointed. There will be days where we don't understand God's plan. There will be days when we cannot stop the tears from flowing. We will have those days, and that is okay. The key is not getting stuck in sorrow. The key is not getting stuck in despair. The key is not getting stuck in disappointment. Instead, we must pray, press, and praise our way through. We must pray, press, and praise our way to healing. We must pray, press, and praise our way to joy. We must pray, press, and praise our way to victory. We must pray, press, and praise our way to God's presence knowing that there is power in his presence, and it's in his presence that we've got this! You've got this! Why? Greater is he that is within you than he that is in the world.

Your situation may be great but know that God is greater. Because HE lives, you can and will make it through this.

Dear God,

My situation is difficult, and I want to give up. Lord help me to draw closer to you. I realize that I cannot do this on my own, so I give this situation over to you. Strengthen me, heal me, and guide me as I press to your presence. Amen.

DAY 5
PRAISING GOD THROUGH THE PAIN

New Year's had quickly made an appearance, and I found myself in deep reflection. One year ago, I was excited about family, friends, work, good health, faith, romance, and much more. Life was great, and I could not wait for what was to come. Fast forward a year and so many of the things that had me floating on cloud nine were now just distant memories.

This past year truly was an example of how we should appreciate what we have for it could be here one minute and gone the next. In this period of reflection, I was surprised to see just how much my life had changed over the course of 365 days. I was surprised to see just how much I had changed.

While I was slowly journeying down the road to emotional healing, physical healing was becoming a necessity. The pain that paused life briefly in October had intensified over the months and eased its way into nearly every moment of my daily routine. This wasn't simply a "let me take an aspirin" and get going type of pain. Instead, it was a halting feeling that demanded all my attention. As its visits increased, it was accompanied by debilitating headaches, numbness in various parts of my body, tingling, and muscle tightness.

The things that I once took for granted were now difficult to do without wanting to shed tears. I never dreamed that walking, playing with my daughter, or even cooking would present such a challenge. Honestly, if I believed that I could have made a living from beneath my blanket, I surely would have tried. Since that was not an option in my profession, I pressed forward.

I remember waking up one Saturday instantly in pain and without any feeling in my arm. Though fear was trying to overtake me, I began to thank God! Do you know what happened next? When I praised God in my pain, my fear began to flee! In addition to that, I was overflowing with peace.

As a parent you try to shield your children from certain things. My health situation was one that I kept to myself, because I didn't want my daughter worrying about things she didn't understand. I thought I was doing a great job, but my little one was more observant that I gave her credit. A few moments after I got out of bed, Trin slowly entered my room. She had an inquisitive look, and the tears were visibly welling up in her eyes. Before I could ask her what was wrong, she said "Mommy, I know you are in pain, but I heard you thanking God. How can you thank God when you are in pain?"

Some of you may be asking the same thing. How can I praise God when I am in pain? Well, my friend,

I will share with you what I shared with my daughter. Although I was hurting and could not feel my arm, I felt better than I had the day before. Though it was small, God had given me a victory, and I was thankful!

Instead of seeing all that was wrong, I placed my focus on and rejoiced about what was going right. We must learn to recognize and appreciate our victories great and small!

The experience with Trinity taught me a very important lesson. Whether it's an 8-year-old concerned about her mother, a coworker, a family member, or a friend; people are watching. They may never say a word, but people are looking to see how we respond to various trials in life. It is important to remember that our reaction to trials could be what draws someone to God or what turns them away because our response shows whether we are walking the walk or simply talking the talk.

Our willingness to praise God in the midst of what we are going through shows our faith in His ability to move in our situation.

No matter what you are facing today, I encourage you to PRAISE your way through!

Dear God,

Today I am finding it difficult to push through the pain. I thank you for all that you have done and all you will do. Help me to continue to have an attitude of praise despite what I am going through. Lord, I know that you love me and are with me through it all. Amen.

"I will bless the Lord at all times. His praise will continuously be in my mouth." Psalm 34:1

DAY 6
HIS PRESENCE

With the increase in pain, seeing the doctor suddenly became part of my new normal. My prayer was that the solution would be simple, and I would be feeling back to my old self in no time. When my primary couldn't figure out what was wrong and referred me to a neurologist, alarm bells starting ringing and any hope of a "simple" fix faded away. I was scheduled to undergo a series of MRI scans to obtain some explanation for this sudden onset of symptoms. My heart was racing, and my hands were shaking as I slowly entered the machine. I thought about quitting but was reminded to hold on and have faith. For two hours, Mark endured the deafening noise of the machine as he sat by my side offering comforting words and support. Each time I wanted to give up, the gentle squeeze from his hand to mine reassured me that everything would be okay. A few weeks later, I went back to the neurologist and heard what seemed to be a fictional term.

"Pseudotumor Cerebri."

"Pseudo...what?", I asked.

"Based on some of your symptoms, I think you may have Pseudotumor Cerebri. This is a condition that mimics a tumor by applying pressure to the brain. We can't be sure without further testing."

Before moving to the second stage of testing, I was prescribed a medication that is commonly used with this condition to manage pain and potentially relieve symptoms.

Over the past year, I spent so much time broken and hurting because I tried to bandage my wounds instead of addressing the source of my pain. Was I now supposed to waste more time suffering with physical pain and using medicine to mask the symptoms? Thankfully, my previous experience provided me with enough clarity that I simply refused to make that mistake again. It was time out for letting my situation control my life. I was ready to take action!

Driving home from the appointment, I was reminded of one of my favorite Bible stories. I thought about the perseverance shown in Luke by the nameless woman who spent 12 years of her life suffering with an issue of blood. She spent all she had and went to every doctor around but never found any relief. Then one day Jesus was passing by, and a fire was ignited within her soul. She wanted a change and was determined to let nothing stop her from reaching Jesus.

What an awesome act of faith! Remembering her story inspired me, and I decided to press. Despite what I had gone through and was going through, I was prepared to press to His presence. I sat in my car and cried out to the Lord, "I need you. I am sick and tired of being SICK AND TIRED! I know that if I can just touch the hem of your garment, then I will be made whole. It doesn't matter what is in front of me. It doesn't matter what is behind me. Touching you Jesus is all that matters because I want to be made whole!"

Some of you may be in a similar place. Perhaps you have been struggling with a situation for days, weeks, months or maybe even years. You have tried everything, and your situation hasn't gotten better, but instead it has gotten worse.

Today there is HOPE! Jesus is passing by, but your desire for change must be greater than your fear of what lies ahead of you. Say that with me: "MY DESIRE FOR CHANGE HAS TO BE GREATER THAN MY FEAR OF WHAT LIES AHEAD OF ME."

Do you want to be made whole?

Then like the woman with the issue of blood, you must become desperate for His presence knowing that there lies your healing, breakthrough, peace, and joy!

Dear God,

I have been struggling with this situation for so long. I don't want to continue doing things my way. I want to do things your way. Lord I am trusting that you can and will make me whole. Amen.

"Daughter, your faith has healed you. Go in peace and be freed from your suffering." Luke 8:48

DAY 7
BE STILL

The alarm sounded at 6:00am and hitting the snooze button was not an option. Today was an extremely important day but one I had been dreading for the past two weeks. All other options had been exhausted, and I finally had to face the "further testing" the doctor had previously mentioned. I arrived at the hospital ready to get in and get out, but that was just silly thinking on my part. As they wheeled me away for my spinal tap, I gave a reassuring smile to my mother and my daughter whose stares could not possibly see the fear that penetrated my heart.

After the procedure was over, I was instructed to lay flat for the next 24 hours. How great of a challenge this was going to be! As the possibilities of what the tests may reveal tried to creep into my mind, I asked the Lord to help me be still. Even though I was unable to physically move, I needed God to calm my spirit and allow me to be still in Him. In that time of stillness, I read several scriptures that ministered to me, removed anxiety, strengthened me, and provided great peace.

As I read them, I was reminded of God's promises and his faithfulness. May these verses encourage you as they did me.

1) "Fear not for I am with you; Be not dismayed, for I am your God. I will strengthen you, Yes, I will help you. I will uphold you with my righteous hand." Isaiah 41:10

Even in our most difficult situations, we have nothing to fear because God has promised to be with us. He also promised to strengthen, help, and uphold us.

2) "God is our refuge and strength, always ready to help in times of trouble." Psalm 46:1

In this verse God is not only promising to be our strength, but he promises to also shelter us from danger or trouble.

3) "Cast your cares on him, because He cares for you." 1 Peter 5:7

This verse is a reminder of God's love for us. He doesn't want us to carry these burdens. He instructs us in His word to give our burdens to Him, trusting that HE is able.

Maybe you're experiencing a situation where you are unsure of the outcome, and the uncertainty has you feeling helpless, worried, and fearful. Do not be afraid is written in the Bible 365 times. That is a daily reminder to live every day FEARLESS.

I challenge you to step away from distractions and allow yourself to be still. In your time of stillness, study God's word and begin to declare His promises over your life.

Dear God,

In this moment where fear is trying to take hold of my heart, help me to be still and stand on your promises. Lord you said that you would be with me, strengthen me, and guide me. I am leaning and depending on you. God please remove any doubt and fear and replace it with joy and peace. Amen.

DAY 8
I AM COMING OUT

As a child, one of my favorite parts of birthday celebrations was blowing out the candles and making a wish. It was an exhilarating experience as you thought of all the possible things you could wish for and how happy you would be when they came true. Oh, how I WISH that wishes actually came true. If they did, I would have definitely wished away the news that was awaiting me on the evening of January 25, 2017.

It was a few days after my procedure, and I began having adverse effects. I was instructed to visit the emergency room to ensure that everything was okay. While there, I experienced the typical poking and prodding that bruised my veins and made me eager to stay away from hospitals. I was told that I needed fluids to replenish what was taken during the spinal tap. As I was waiting, the doctor said he would request the results of the procedure. I was a little nervous but remembered the adage "No news is good news." Surely, if something was wrong, my neurologist would have contacted me by now.

What seemed like an eternity later, the doctor entered the room and sat down. My heart dropped, and I instantly knew something was wrong, yet I still wasn't prepared for what I was about to hear. "I am sorry to say that you have M.S."

I was in complete shock and knew not what to say. I tried to control my tears as the nurse followed up by telling me that treatments have advanced, and I could still live an okay life. When I got inside of my car, all I could do was scream. I called my mom and could hear her holding back tears as she tried to console her baby girl. She offered words of encouragement, but nothing she could say would take away the all too familiar feeling of hurt that was quickly overwhelming me.

For the next week I walked around feeling broken, discouraged, and defeated. How could this be happening? Why was this happening? What was I doing wrong?

While wallowing in a sea of tears, I received a text from my friend, Ryanne. She knew nothing about the fear that was racing through my mind, yet her words spoke directly to my situation. I realized that God was speaking to me and instantly knew I had a choice to make. I was either going to dwell in this pit of despair and let this diagnosis defeat me or I was going to trust God and PRAISE MY WAY OUT!

Whatever you are facing today, I challenge you to trust God and PRAISE YOUR WAY OUT!

Praise your way out knowing that your praise is a weapon. Praise your way out knowing that God is able to do exceedingly and abundantly above all you could ask or hope for. Praise your way out knowing if He did it before, He can and will do it again. Praise your way out knowing what's broken can be restored and what's empty can be filled. Praise your way out knowing that He is your rock, your strength, your refuge, your healer, and your redeemer. Praise your way out knowing that greater is He that is within you than he that is in the world. Praise your way out knowing that God is bigger than this situation.

If it isn't obvious, I decided to praise my way out. It is important to remember that praise precedes the victory. When we remember this, we can experience joy knowing that it doesn't come from the world but from God and God alone.

When you PRAISE your way through trials, you make a declaration to the world that says, "No matter what comes my way, I still have joy, and I AM COMING OUT OF THIS THING!"

Dear God,
Thank you! Thank you for who you are in my life. Thank you for all you have done and all I know you will do. The road ahead may be rough, but I thank you for being with me. Thank you for giving me the victory. Amen.

DAY 9
STANDING ON HIS PROMISES

When my heart is feeling overwhelmed, lead me to the rock that is higher than I. David's words never rang so true as I discovered the Rock provided me with a sense of safety and security when the world around me seemed to be under attack.

In the weeks that followed my diagnosis, I was still trying to wrap my head around this shocking, life altering news. I spent a great amount of time contemplating the future and praying to make the right decisions. What would be the best course of treatment? What doctor/facility should oversee my care? When do I tell my family? What does the road ahead look like?

I also started researching because learning everything about this disease that had made its way into my life was now a priority. At the top of my list was discovering the impact it could have on me and that sweet, precious little girl that I call my heart. I joined online support groups, searched exercises, and printed meal plans to prevent flare ups. If there was something M.S. related to be found, I was looking.

I realized that I had a huge fight ahead in many ways, so I did everything possible to prepare for battle. One of the most important things that I did each day was study the word. The word served as a source of strength and encouragement, and it gave me a daily reminder of God's promises and provided instruction on how to fight back against the feelings of doubt, fear, anxiety, and depression.

Fighting back was critical as it prevented me from sinking back into that deep, dark hole of emptiness and hopelessness that was my home for so many months. When I began to feel overwhelmed, I called out to God in PRAYER. Attempting to fight this battle on my own was as though I was on sinking sand; therefore, I placed my foot on the Solid Rock knowing that it was God and only God that could sustain me. God's promises became my foundation as I knew that I could trust and depend on His word. Each day I read the following scriptures and started declaring my healing.

Exodus 15:26
"I am the Lord God that healeth thee."

Psalm 118:17
"I shall not die but live and proclaim what the Lord has done."

Psalm 147:3
"He heals the brokenhearted and binds up their wounds."

Jeremiah 17:14

"Heal me, O Lord, and I shall be healed; save me, and I shall be saved, for You are my praise."

Isaiah 53:5

"But He was pierced for our transgressions, He was crushed for our iniquities; the punishment that brought us peace was on Him, and by His wounds we are healed."

For those of you that need physical healing, I encourage you to read these scriptures and stand on the promises of God. Go to the rock, Jesus, and activate that unwavering, unshakable, mountain moving faith, and declare your healing today.

Dear God,

I need healing today. Despite how things may look or how I may feel, I am standing on your word. As I look to you, help me to have immovable faith. Just like the tree planted by the water, I shall not be moved. YOU oh Lord are my healer, and I thank you. Amen.

DAY 10
NOT TODAY

A s a child, my mom was a superhero in my eyes able to fix anything that was broken. From boo boos to broken hearts, she would always have a solution. As much as she wanted to, it saddened us both to know that my lifelong superhero was not able to fix this situation. What she would give me would be one of the greatest "fixes" of my life. She provided me with spiritual guidance and encouragement that would give me the strength to fight back against a crafty enemy.

One quiet morning, I opened my eyes at the harmonious ringing coming from my phone signaling an email had arrived. I opened the email thinking it would be the normal forwarded message or request to proofread. Instead, it was a familiar verse that would equip me for the road ahead. The verse was found in Ephesians 6:10-12:

"Be strong in the Lord and in his mighty power. Put on all of God's armor so that you will be able to stand firm against all strategies of the devil.

For we are not fighting against flesh and blood enemies, but against evil rulers and authorities of the unseen world, against mighty powers in this dark world, and against evil spirits in the heavenly places."

I have read that verse dozens of times, but this day it was as though I was reading it with new eyes.

It is important for us to remember that the enemy doesn't play fair because he is on a mission to seek, kill, and destroy. Just as God knows our weaknesses so does the enemy, and he will use those areas to attack. As you all know, my weakness as of late had been physical and emotional pain. Receiving this news about my health stirred up so many emotions; and on top of that, there were many days where my pain level was at a twenty.

The next morning, the pain was so unbearable that I wanted to go to the hospital. The enemy was coming at me hard and trying to plant seeds of fear and doubt. He wanted me to believe that life as I knew it was over, joy was a thing of the past, and that I would not survive. He wanted me to simply throw up my hands and give up.

If I had never prepared myself mentally and spiritually for this fight, it would have been very easy for me to fall apart. To be honest, a year earlier I would have done just that, but instead I suited up in the full armor of God and prepared for battle.

I pressed my way forward knowing that giving up was not an option. I pressed my way forward knowing that I serve a God who can do ALL things. I pressed my way forward knowing that I am more than a conquer through Him who loves me. With this in mind, I boldly began declaring:

NOT TODAY SATAN!
NOT TODAY!
YOU WILL NOT STEAL MY JOY!
YOU WILL NOT STEAL MY PEACE!
YOU WILL NOT STEAL MY STRENGTH!

We have to stop giving the enemy power in our lives when God has already given us the victory. We must walk in our God given victory knowing that our hope is not in man. Our hope is not in ourselves. Our hope is not in our situation.

Our hope is in the ONE. Our hope is the GREAT I AM. Our hope is in the ALPHA AND THE OMEGA. Our hope is in the LILY IN THE VALLEY, the BRIGHT and MORNING STAR. Our hope is in the PRINCE OF PEACE.

Our hope is in the one who was wounded our transgressions, bruised for our iniquities. The chastisement of our peace was upon his back and by His stripes, WE ARE HEALED!

Our hope is the one who has proven himself FAITHFUL. Our hope is in the one who LOVES US with an everlasting love. Our hope is in the one who said he would NEVER LEAVE NOR FORSAKE US. Our hope is in the one who has ALWAYS STOOD BY OUR SIDE. Our hope is in the EVERLASTING GOD!

Put on the full armor of God so that you are able to STAND! Know that you are not in this battle alone because the word says, "When the enemy comes in like a flood, God will lift up a standard against him." There will be days when life hits you hard, but be strong in the Lord, declare victory, and tell the enemy NOT TODAY!

DAY 11
SPEAK LIFE

Friday is my favorite day of the week because it symbolizes the start of the weekend. Ah the weekend, a time of rest, relaxation, and fun; I absolutely love the weekend. While I am usually excited for Friday, this particular day had me dreading what was ahead.

The bell rang at its normal time indicating it was time for me to go. While I would normally start packing my bag and humming my favorite tune, I found myself glued to my desk grading papers. It wasn't the usual or sometimes surprising stress of work that had me in this mood, nor was it the pressure and responsibility of home life. It was the fact that my week now included intense physical therapy on Monday, Wednesday, and Friday.

As I drove across the street to the office, I started telling myself all the reasons I did not want to engage in therapy. "I am still sore from Wednesday's session. Therapy isn't going to change my diagnosis.

This is just a temporary fix to a permanent problem. What happens when I can no longer go to therapy?" I finally just blurted out, "I can't do this today! I just can't!"

Then in an instant, a still small voice whispered, "Why not?" I stopped trying to convince myself of reasons to quit and realized that I was speaking defeat over my situation before even beginning the battle.

Often, we experience things in life and find it easy to say that we "cannot do something" or we "don't know how" we are going to make it through a situation. We become defeated because we have chosen to speak negativity, and in doing so we rob ourselves of joy and peace. Well today, I challenge to you to speak life!

It is imperative for us to speak life into our situations and surround ourselves with positive people who are willing and able to do the same. You can't speak death or allow people to speak negativity into your life and expect things to grow. "Why?", you wonder. "What difference do words make?", you ask. The Bible tells us that the power of life and death lies in the tongue, so the things that we speak can manifest themselves into our lives.

No matter what you are facing, speak life into your situation! You may be feeling sick. Speak life: "By His stripes I am healed." Someone says You can't. Speak life: "I can do all things through Christ who strengthens me." The doctor says there's nothing they can do. Speak life: "I shall not die but live and declare the works of the Lord." The enemy tries to remind you of who you used to be. Speak life: "It doesn't matter who you say that I am. I am who GOD says that I am."

Stop letting doubt and fear rob you of joy and peace. Stop being defeated when God has called you victorious. What you say is just as powerful as what you do. God has given you power. It's up to you to use it, so again I challenge you to SPEAK LIFE!

Dear God,
Help me to put my trust in you. Regardless of what lies ahead, help me to speak life. Amen.

DAY 12
GOD IS

"Not my will, but thy will be done" were the words I kept repeating on that warm April morning. It was around 6:00am, and I was more than ready to get the day started. I got Trinity ready, packed up the car, and began the two-and-a-half-hour trip that was ahead of us. Today was the day I had been anticipating since January 25th. Today was the day that I would get a second opinion and determine a course of treatment. I was filled with a variety of emotions, but one thing was certain, I just wanted answers.

Around 9:00am we arrived at the massive Johns Hopkins campus, and my nerves were getting the best of me. My heart was hoping one thing, yet my mind was preparing me for another. Entering the facility, the check in area seemed more like airport security than a doctor's office. The waiting area was filled with so many people fighting battles far worse than I could imagine. In that moment, my problems seemed so insignificant compared to theirs.

I was called back to begin lab work which resulted in me being skittish of needles to this day. After testing, I entered the exam room and met with the doctor. He did a lengthy series of test, and his pauses made me nervous. His request that I repeat movements had me on edge. Fear was beginning to rise up, but instead of allowing myself to fall apart, I began reminding myself of who God is.

God is faithful
God is loving
God is my rock
God is my strength
God is my protector
God is my hope
God is my peace
God is my joy
God is my all and all

When we are in the heart of the storm with the end not in sight, sometimes it is very easy to be distracted by the winds and the waves that are trying to overtake us. The conditions of our situation seem great and mighty and attempt to instill fear in our hearts. When we are fearful, victory seems impossible. When we are fearful, peace seems unattainable. When we are fearful, joy is non-existent.

Remember the disciples? They witnessed Jesus perform a multitude of miracles, but the moment a great tempest arose, they were afraid they would perish. They were in a panic and went to Jesus, questioning if he cared that they were going to die. Some of us are like the disciples, so quick to question God's love for us the moment we have to endure.

Even in their lack of faith, God proved himself faithful and calmed the storm. It was then that the disciples proclaimed who God was.

The doctor reentered the room, and I braced myself for what he was about to say.

"Looking over your chart and after your exam, I do not feel that you have M.S. You should continue physical therapy and continue seeing your neurologist to see how to move forward."

I was overjoyed and relieved by the news that I did not have this disease that devastated me months prior. It was the news that I had been waiting for; however, I still did not know what was causing my symptoms. Not knowing can be extremely difficult, yet I was at peace. My journey was far from over, but I went forth in faith proclaiming God is my healer!

In your time of uncertainty, activate your faith and declare who God is in your life. Yes, the situation you're facing may be great, but God is greater!

Dear God,

When the storms of life are raging, help me to find peace in you. No matter how it looks, help me to remember that if you can calm the winds and the angry sea, then you can surely fix all that is troubling me. Amen.

DAY 13
JOY

To say that once I left Hopkins everything was back to normal and my health was fully restored would be a dream come true. Unfortunately, I was not able to make that declaration because the reality was that my days were spent fighting through numbness, tingling, headaches, muscle tightness, and intense pain. I went to multiple specialists, endured a few more blood sticks, and still did not have a definitive answer. The only solution given was medicine to help manage the pain.

This storm had been raging in my life for so long, and I felt like I was now in my midnight hour. You know, the time when you are all alone, everyone and everything around you is still, and you are left alone with your thoughts. The thoughts that say, "how long is this storm going to last?" The thoughts that say, "what is wrong and why can't anyone figure it out?". The thoughts that lead to feelings of sadness and frustration. In those times when depression roared like a ravenous lion, I found myself doing something outside of my norm. I began singing the songs that my grandmother used to sing in church. I closed my eyes, lifted my hands, and sang to God, "It is well with my soul." I realized that focusing on the problem was not getting me closer to a solution. Crying about the pain and the lack of answers was not making things better. In actuality, it was stressing me out and making things much worse. How do we find joy in the midnight hour? We PRAISE!!!

Many people may feel that praising God during trials is a difficult task, but it is truly an act of faith. Let's examine the story of Paul and Silas found in Acts 16. Paul and Silas found themselves imprisoned for sharing the Gospel. They had been beaten, thrown into the inner dungeon, and their hands and feet were bound. Now, Paul and Silas could have worried about all that was going wrong, but instead of focusing on the suffering, they called on the Savior! In their midnight hour, Paul and Silas prayed and sang praises to God. This serves as a powerful reminder that we should not let anything hinder our praise!

They prayed and opened the lines of communication with God knowing that it was only Him that could change their situation. In what most would consider bleak circumstances, Paul and Silas were able to find joy through prayer and praise. Their actions in the face of adversity greatly exemplified faith and love.

As a result of their praise, the atmosphere shifted, and God began to move. The Bible says that suddenly there was a great earthquake that shook the foundations of the prison. Then all the doors were opened, and all their bands were loosed! This is another great reminder that circumstances should not determine our praise, but our praise determines our circumstances. In other words, there is power in PRAISE!

In your midnight hour, connect to God through PRAYER and PRAISE knowing that He hears you, and He cares. Find peace and reassurance in God's love for you.

I have found comfort in knowing that even at my lowest point, God is at his best. Even at my lowest, God is still THE best. If I have THE BEST loving and looking out for me, then why should I worry? Why should you worry? Regardless of what lies ahead of you, find joy in God. You may not know the how or the when, but you should know without a doubt that God CAN and WILL deliver! That, my friends, is something to rejoice about!

Dear God,

Lord I thank you for giving me joy and peace in the midst of what I am going through. When doubt and fear attempt to surface in my life, give me a heart and a mind to praise my way through. Amen.

DAY 14
LETTING GO

When I was five years old, my grandmother bought me a doll from my favorite cartoon show, Rainbow Bright. Everywhere I went, Rainbow went. As I grew older and acquired new favorites, Rainbow Bright still held a special place in my heart. Time passed and as I was preparing to head off to college, my mom and I were packing up my room. My eyes were like saucers when I noticed she had put Rainbow in the box labeled trash. Her argument that I hadn't played with the doll in years was certainly valid, yet there was something inside me that didn't want to let go.

For a reason not yet revealed, I was placed in a situation where I had no clue what was causing my symptoms, pain was still a daily occurrence, and doctors had no solid diagnosis. I was frustrated at the lack of answers and the amount of time that my life had been in such an uproar. My present picture had become void of stability, and the future was a sea of uncertainty. This created a feeling of uneasiness and caused me to desperately seek some sense of normalcy. Achieving this goal would require me to do the very thing that frightened me eighteen years earlier.

Relinquishing control was scary, but I knew it was necessary. I had tried doing things my way and gained nothing other than frustration and brokenness. It was time for me to let God take control. Letting go is certainly not easy because it requires something that most of us are not willing to give…TRUST! When seeking direction, I find that many people often share the scripture "Trust in the Lord with all your heart, and lean not to your own understanding," but I wonder how many actually follow what it says. How many of us TRUST God with all our heart? Trust is an easy task when you're in good health, the kids are doing well, the job is a source of enjoyment, the marriage is spectacular, and life is going just as you planned.

What about those days when life is anything but great? What about those moments when the kids are acting crazy, the job is beyond stressful, and the spouse is getting on your last nerve? What about when you've been unemployed for months, you just lost that bundle of joy you'd been praying for, your heart is broken, your marriage is falling apart, or your loved one is fighting for their life? When life throws curveball after curveball, can you still trust God?

Crying through the pain, I knew that I had to trust God like never before. I couldn't simply give him part of the situation, but I needed to let go of all the doubt, fear, and uncertainty that had invaded my spirit and taken over my life since my symptoms began. Though I did not have answers from the doctor, I trusted in God's promises and knew my healing would be according to His WILL and His WAY and done in His TIMING. I no longer needed to know how he would deliver, nor did I need to know when it would happen. I went forth simply BELIEVING that it would happen!

You may be facing what appears to be an impossible situation, but today I challenge you to let go and TRUST God. If you find yourself questioning how you can trust God in your current situation, then I would like to share these reminders:

Abraham and Sarah had to trust God to fulfill the promise of their child.

Joseph had to trust God as he was sold into slavery by his own brothers and later imprisoned for something that he did not do.

David had to trust God as he went into battle against a giant!

Shadrach, Meshach, and Abendego had to trust God as they were thrown into a fiery furnace.

Daniel had to trust God as he was placed in a den of lions.

Job had to trust God as he lost his family, home, friends, and his health.

If God delivered Abraham, Sarah, Joseph, David, Shadrach, Meshach, Abendego, Daniel, and Job, then he can surely deliver you!

Dear God,

In what seems to be impossible, help me to lean and depend on you knowing that you are able to make the impossible, possible. Lord you know what is best for me. Help me to trust you with ALL my heart and lean not to my own understanding. Amen.

DAY 15
WORSHIP IS A WEAPON

My declaration of faith was not made without encountering some strong opposition. Foolishly, I didn't realize that my faith was going to be tested so quickly. The seven days that followed were intense to say the least. I was in pain day in and day out, and issues were arising at work and in my personal life. Things seemed to be falling apart. On the seventh day, there was an issue with my car. It was something very minor, but combined with everything else that was taking place, it became the "final straw". The enemy heard my promise to trust God like never before, and he was working overtime to test the sincerity of those words.

Can you relate? Have you ever felt like the storms of life were raging uncontrollably? Have you felt like you were being bombarded with trial after trial? Have you ever felt like you were at your wits end? Have you ever felt that throwing in the towel was far simpler than throwing up your hands?

That is the road that I was traveling. However, instead of getting frustrated and allowing the situation to steal the things that I cherished, I entered into the presence of God and began to worship. I sat alone in my car, turned on the music, and proceeded to thank God for all he had done in my life. I began praising God and declaring His promises over my life:

"Lord you are Jehovah Jireh. Thank you for providing for me. Lord you are Jehovah Rapha. Thank you for healing me. Lord you are Jehovah Shalom. Thank you for giving me peace. Lord you are Jehovah Ra-ah. Thank you for keeping me."

Tears were flowing as I thought about how faithful God had been to me and my family. I was so filled up thinking about his goodness, his grace, and his mercy. I was ecstatic thinking about how he loved me, and I cried out to him with complete adoration, "Lord I love you!" As I worshiped, the atmosphere began to shift. All those feelings that the enemy was trying to stir up faded away, and I was overflowing with feelings of peace, positivity, hope, and happiness.

Worship is a powerful weapon because it places us in the presence of God, and amazing things happen in His presence. In His presence, the wounded are made whole. In His presence, sight is restored to the blind man and the lame man leaps for joy. In His presence, hardened hearts are melted, minds are renewed, and lives are transformed. In His presence, people find freedom. Amazing things happen in the presence of God!

Your current situation may be more than you can handle, and it is pushing you to your breaking point. Today I encourage you to throw up your hands in worship and allow God to move in your life.

Dear God,

Thank you for your grace, your tender mercy, and your unfailing love. Thank you for loving and looking out for me. Lord you are good, and you are faithful. I love you Lord. Amen.

DAY 16
WAITING ON THE LORD

This past year and a half has been extremely challenging and taught me things about myself that I never realized. I discovered that I spoke often about faith, but I failed to exercise faith in my daily life. Instead, I allowed my sight and feelings to leave me discouraged and defeated.

Although the circumstances involving my health caused me to grow in ways I never imagined, there were still days where I found myself constantly wondering when my healing would occur. I knew God was going to heal me, but I wanted it to happen quickly. I wanted it to happen NOW. I was growing tired of waiting because it was unbearable and unpleasant.

I was driving home from work and trying to decide on what to do for dinner. It was about 6:30pm; I had papers to grade, homework to check, and preparations to make for the next day. My mind was focused on "quick and easy" because I did not want to wait in lines at stores or wait for dinner to be done before starting my other tasks. Funny thing is that God used something as simple as dinner to teach me how important waiting truly is.

In the middle of my commute home I received the message "What's quick and easy is not always best." Initially that was hard for me to conceive because we live in a microwave society where instant gratification is the expected, but it is not reality. As much as I wanted to, I couldn't snap my fingers and receive healing. I had to learn to wait on the Lord. YOU must learn to wait on the Lord.

Waiting is not our first choice because as we wait life goes on. Other things begin to happen in our lives and in the lives of those around us, and we get discouraged as we wonder when and if God's promises are going to be fulfilled.

"I have been waiting for this promise for a long time, and it hasn't happened yet. God can't still deliver after all this time, right?" We've all had those thoughts at one point or another. We need to remember that God is not a man that he should lie, so if God said it, know that it will happen! We also need to remember that God will show up in His time, and He is with us even in the waiting.

What are you waiting for? Better yet, what are you TRUSTING God for? Maybe you are like Abraham and Sarah, waiting for the day that you hold your son or daughter in your arms. WAIT ON HIM. Maybe you are like the woman with the issue of blood in need of a healing. WAIT ON HIM. Maybe you are like the father of the prodigal son, waiting for that lost loved one to come to Christ. WAIT ON HIM. Wait on Him, knowing that God knows what you need and when you need it. Romans 8:28 tells us that ALL things work together for the good of those who love the Lord and are called according to his purpose.

Waiting may be difficult, but we need to stay focused on God. Don't get distracted by the bumps in the road. Don't get enticed by what appears to be easy. Don't get upset because the promise isn't coming as quickly as you think it should come. Wait on the Lord, and trust that He knows best. Yes, you may have been waiting for what seems to be a long time. Abraham, Sarah, Joseph, Moses, and even Jesus waited. It wasn't easy for them, but they did it and so can you. Trust that in God's time He WILL deliver. In the meantime, continue to stand on his promises and praise him for what is to come knowing that it may not be quick, it may not be easy, but it is worth the wait!

Dear God,
Help me to wait on you in spite of what I see and in spite of how I feel. You know what I need, and I trust in your timing. Let me not be discouraged but instead give me a thankful heart. Amen.

DAY 17
WHY NOT?

Autumn's breeze greeted me as I headed out to work. As I exhaled the cool air, I realized that something significant had occurred. Not only had God blessed me with a new job full of great, supportive people, but October 2017 had arrived and with it marked one year since the onset of my symptoms. It marked one year of struggling with a problem that seemed to have no name, yet I was thankful. Not only was I thankful, but I was joyful!

That afternoon, I decided to share my testimony with others through my social media devotionals. I wanted to let the world know just how good God had been to me throughout the course of this past year. Since December of 2016, I had been sharing weekly devotionals, but this one felt different because it required me to be vulnerable and divulge thoughts, feelings, and situations that I had not shared with many people. Nervously, I sat in my car, hit the live button, and gave my testimony. Afterwards, I had several people question why I was celebrating even though I had no diagnosis and more importantly no cure. I sat quietly for a moment and then repeated their question aloud, "How can I celebrate when I don't have a diagnosis or a cure?" After hearing those words, I instantly smiled and said, "why not?!"

Why couldn't I thank God for the victories that he had given me throughout this year? Why couldn't I thank God for comforting me when I was hurting? Why couldn't I thank God for giving me strength when all I wanted to do was quit? Why couldn't I thank God for giving me peace when my body was giving me nothing but pain and anguish? Why couldn't I thank God for providing me with people to encourage and uplift me when I needed it most? Why couldn't I thank God for giving me pain free hours, days, and now weeks? Why couldn't I thank God for his love and his goodness? Why not?

Let me ask you a question. If you walked into a football stadium and everyone sat quietly until the end of the 4th quarter, what would you think? Chances are you would probably think you were being pranked on a hidden camera show or you landed into some alternate universe, right? After all, cheering a team to victory is what is expected.

All too often, we tend to wait until the end of the "4th quarter" before we begin to praise God. My question is, why? Is God only good on the mountaintop? Is God only good when the battle is finally over? Of course not!

I remember being in church as a child and singing the words of an old hymn "Morning by morning new mercies I see. All I have needed, thy hands have provided. Great is thy faithfulness, Lord unto me." I didn't really understand the magnitude of those words until my adult life, but oh how true they are. God provides everything that we need to make it through this journey. He showers us with new mercies every single day, and He is faithful even when we are faithless.

Whether it's a pain free day, a hot meal or refreshing drink, a phone call for an interview, an unexpected text that lifts your spirit, an A on a test, a well-behaved class, an extra hour of sleep, a call to say I love you, or an answered prayer...THANK GOD!

We must recognize and appreciate the victories that we receive daily knowing that each small victory is bringing us one step closer to our overall triumph. Don't wait until the storm is over to shout, but instead learn to dance in the rain.

Dear God,

Thank you for the victories that you give to me each day. Help me to see and appreciate those blessings great and small. Teach me to have an attitude of praise before, during, and after the storm. Amen.

DAY 18
TOO FAR

December flew in bringing chilly temperatures and beautiful scenery. I was extremely excited because Christmas is my favorite time of year, and I was now going on three months of being pain free! Excitement was a feeling that I had not felt in a long time, and now I couldn't get enough of it. Life was going great, and finally being on the mountaintop felt even greater. During my time on this earth, life has taught me several things: time waits for no one, trouble doesn't last always, and after the mountaintop comes the valley.

I headed into work one morning eager to teach and inspire. It was also the week of winter break, so I had an extra pep in my step as I knew a time of rest and relaxation was ahead. Before I entered my classroom, I received some news that hit me like a ton of bricks. The news was unexpected and something I never anticipated, so needless to say that I was floored. How could this be happening now?

In an instant, the signs I know too well began to surface. The once bright and sunny sky became gray and ominous. The winds began to intensify and raindrops of fear, doubt, and worry, were beginning to fall from the sky. A great storm was coming my way, but what was I to do?

Should I fall back into the pit of despair? Should I be overcome with worry? Should I allow doubt and fear to defeat me? Should I allow this current storm to rob me of the joy and peace that I fought so hard to achieve? My friends, the answer to those questions is an astounding NO! The reason is very simple, I had come TOO FAR to turn back! Yes, the situation was upsetting. Yes, the road ahead was going to be difficult. Yes, I was yet again in another storm, but it was not worth relinquishing my joy and my peace. God brought me TOO FAR for me to turn back. Retreating was not an option, so I did the two things I knew how to do. I PRAYED and PRAISED.

You may find yourself in a similar place. You may be wondering how in the world you can be in the valley again when you were just on the mountaintop. How can a storm be raging when you barely had time to enjoy the sun? Don't get discouraged my brothers and sisters. Don't be tempted to turn around and leave this Christian journey. James 1: 2-4 tells us to "consider it pure joy whenever you face trials of many kinds, because you know that the testing of your faith produces perseverance. Let perseverance finish its work so that you may be mature and complete, not lacking anything."

Think about this question for a moment. Why are farmers thankful for the rain? Farmers know that rain is essential to their success because it prevents drought and produces growth. As Christians, we were never promised a life void of tests and trials. The truth is that we are going to be tried repeatedly in this life, but just like the rain, those trials will produce GROWTH that is essential as we mature in Christ.

Therefore, trials should not steal your joy or leave you bereft of peace. The key is remembering that joy comes from Christ alone. When you realize this, then situations no longer have the ability to steal your happiness.

When storms arise and the rain begins to fall, do not grow weary. Think about what you learned during the last storm. Think about the growth that you have experienced as a result. Now, PRAY and ask God what he is trying to teach you through this test. Ask him to direct you and strengthen you for the journey ahead. Next, PRAISE and thank him for the rain, knowing that it is producing spiritual growth within. Lastly, when the enemy tries to plant seeds of doubt to persuade you to give up, let him know YOU'VE COME TOO FAR TO TURN BACK!

Dear God,
Storm after storm is not easy, but today I thank you for the rain. I thank you for helping me to grow and mature in you. Amen.

DAY 19
GIANTS

As a little girl, I remember reading and watching numerous fairytales. There were stories of a princess locked away in a tall tower, a boy with magic beans, a young girl fighting against her wicked stepmother, or a prince looking to slay a ferocious dragon to save his true love. In every story, the protagonist had to defeat some sort of giant that was standing in the way of happiness. My love for these classics has not diminished as I share them with my daughter; however, I now know that giants do not just exist in fairytales.

The reality is that giants come in all forms, and each of us has a giant of some sort in our lives. Some call their giants depression and anxiety. Others face alcoholism or addiction. Some battle against low self-esteem and loneliness. Others fight against letting go of people, things, or emotions. My giants of late have been fear, sickness, and grief. While identifying giants is an important step, it is even more important to recognize how to defeat the giants that seek to control our lives.

I am reminded of the young shepherd boy who engaged in battle with an opponent that others thought to be daunting. The Philistine warrior, Goliath, stood over nine feet tall and came out for forty days challenging the Israelite army to fight. Goliath's stature and intimidating words terrified the Israelites, and their fear overwhelmed them causing them to flee from battle. Does this sound familiar? Many of us proclaim defeat simply based on how our situation looks. Our fears outweigh our faith when in actuality, our faith should overcome our fears.

David, who had been tending his father's sheep, arrived on the scene and was instantly prepared to go into battle. Since David was a youth with no experience, Saul opposed him fighting a giant who had been a soldier his entire life. David could have looked at his seemingly impossible odds and claimed defeat, but instead he replied, "The Lord who rescued me from the paw of the lion and the paw of the bear will rescue me from the hand of this Philistine."

David's response was a great affirmation of faith! Despite how things looked and despite the opinions of others, David remained FOCUSED on God knowing that it was only God who would provide the victory! David's response is a great reminder for us to keep our eyes on God. When we focus on the problem, we become like the Israelites: overwhelmed, fearful, and defeated; but when we focus on Him, God gives us the strength and the peace to move forward.

When David finally approached Goliath, he was taunted by his opponent. He could have allowed

Goliath's rant to discourage him, create doubt, and cause him to retreat like the Israelites; but instead, David again pressed on in faith saying, "you come to me with a sword and spear and javelin, but I come against you in the name of the Lord God almighty...All those gathered here will know that it is not by sword or spear that the Lord saves; for the battle is the Lord's, and he will give all of you into our hands". David again displayed tremendous faith by declaring victory over his situation. David knew that the battle was won BEFORE stepping onto the battlefield. David knew that victory was not by his actions alone but by his faith in God.

Today, you may be engaged in warfare against a mighty giant. You may feel taunted and overwhelmed by your past, your struggles, and the circumstances of your situation. The situation may seem bleak, and others may feel that your opponent is unstoppable. Do not be afraid, and do not give up! Like David, you must go forth in faith knowing that the giant in front of you is not bigger than the God inside of you! Go forth in faith knowing that Jesus is your giant slayer! Go forth in faith and declare VICTORY!

Dear God,

Help me understand that this battle is not mine, but it is yours. Help me to put my trust in you and be still as you fight for me. Amen.

DAY 20
YOU'RE COMING OUT

These past two and a half years have been a period of great transformation. Yes, I still miss my aunt daily, but I find peace knowing that pain is not her portion and comfort knowing that I will see her again. Yes, I still experience the symptoms that began in October of 2016, yet I know that I am healed. Yes, I know that more storms will surface, yet I am not afraid.

February 12, 2016 marked the beginning of a very trying time in my life, but it also took me on a journey to true faith. I was engulfed in a great storm that seemed it would rage on indefinitely. When I thought that a beacon of light was beginning to surface, the sky darkened as my health was under attack. There were times that I felt as though I had been thrown into the fire without any hope of survival.

Friends, there are two words that can change any situation: BUT GOD. It took me a while to realize it, but God never left my side. He was with me in the midnight hour providing strength and comfort. It was God who brought me out of the darkest period of my life. Like me, you may feel like you are in the fire right now, but I want you to know that YOU ARE COMING OUT!

During this season, I was reminded of the three Hebrew boys that were thrown into the fiery furnace because they stood for what was right. They were placed in a situation where their demise appeared certain. Their enemy viewed them as defeated but failed to realize that these three boys served a God who specializes in the impossible.

The story of the fiery furnace helped me greatly as it is one of remarkable faith in the midst of adversity. It teaches us how to respond to the trials that feel like they are going to overtake us. Here are three lessons from the furnace:

1) **Speak boldly over your situation-** Shadrach, Meshach, and Abendego were facing death but boldly declared their faith in God's ability to deliver them, "If we are thrown into the blazing furnace, the God we serve is able to deliver us from it, and he will deliver us from your hand" (Daniel 3:17). Chances are that this is not your first trial, right? Of course not! Speak the promises of God over your situation with boldness and authority knowing that if He delivered you before, He can deliver you again!

2) **God is with you-** In an ideal world, following Christ would free us from experiencing daily troubles. Though that may be ideal, it is not realistic. We will experience trials, but it is

important to remember that God is right there with us! The Bible tells us that after the boys were thrown into the furnace, Nebuchadnezzar "leaped to his feet in amazement and asked his advisors, 'weren't there three men that we tied up and threw into the furnace?... Look! I see four men walking around the fire... and the fourth looks like a god'" (Daniel 3:24-25). Shadrach, Meshach, and Abendego knew that God was with them, and His presence provided them with peace and the ability to praise. Whatever you are facing today, praise God and find peace in His presence!

3) **You're coming out**- I must admit that this is my favorite part of the story because when Shadrach, Meshach, and Abendego were brought out of the furnace "the fire had not harmed their bodies, nor was a hair of their heads singed; their robes were not scorched, and there was no smell of fire on them" (Daniel 3: 27). What an amazing revelation! Yes, we may go through the fire, but when God brings us out, we will not look like what we have been through!

You're coming out of this test with a testimony that you may declare to others "Oh taste and see that the Lord is good!" You're coming out with the ability to encourage someone else by saying "If it had not been for the Lord on my side, where would I be?" You're coming out with a **but God** praise! "I was in the fire, **but God** kept me. I was weak, **but God** strengthened me. I was down and out, **but**

God picked me up. I was in the storm, **but God** protected me. I was going through, **but God** brought me out. I was lost, **but God** saved me. If He did it for me, He can do it for you!" Sometimes we have to go through the fire to be on fire for God!

You may be in what seems like an impossible situation, but remember that you serve a God that can make the impossible, possible. Do not be discouraged by the duration of your test or by the intensity of the fire. Instead, declare the promises of God and know that He is with you every step of the way. Finally, REJOICE! Rejoice knowing that this too shall pass, and YOU ARE COMING OUT!

DAY 21
PRAY. PRAISE. SLAY. REPEAT.

My cousin, Austin, recently said something that resonated with me. He said, "many people today have sight but no vision." As I sit here reflecting, I realize how those words rang true in my life. When this journey began, my head was spinning with grief, worry, doubt, fear, and tremendous uncertainty. Joy and peace were unattainable because I could not envision myself on the other side of my situation. How did I make it? How did I survive the greatest storm of my life? GOD! God changed my vision and my mindset in the most unexpected way.

In April of 2017, God gave me a vision to do something that I had never before considered. I woke up one morning with multiple designs flowing through my head and itching to be brought to life. Soon after, Next Level Faith Apparel was born. One of the first designs created that April morning is the very premise of this book. It was a shirt with the message "PRAY. PRAISE. SLAY. REPEAT." Those four words changed my life and taught me how to encounter storms without losing joy and peace.

You may have just come out of a storm, you may be engulfed in one currently, or you may see one brewing on the horizon. Do not be alarmed, and do not be afraid. Simply follow these instructions: PRAY, PRAISE, SLAY, AND REPEAT!

PRAY: The first and most critical step when facing storms is to PRAY! I know this is hard for some of us to fathom because we are so quick to phone a friend or a loved one for advice. Many times, when I was feeling down, I would call my mom for sound guidance. While she gave me the best advice possible, it did not take away the pain that I was feeling. It was only when I began talking to God that I noticed a change in my situation, my heart, and my attitude. In Philippians 4 we are told, "Don't worry about anything; instead, PRAY about everything, tell God what you need." Those instructions are very clear and simple. Tell God your doubts and fears. Tell God why you are hurting. Tell God your frustrations. Tell God those things that are stressing you, causing you to shed tears, and keeping you up at night. Seek God and ask him for direction as you are going through this situation. You don't have to endure alone because the Bible says, "Cast your cares on Him because He cares for you" (1 Peter 5:7), so PRAY knowing that God loves you, He cares, and He is the only one that can calm the raging storm in your life.

PRAISE: Philippians 4 continues by encouraging us to "Thank Him for what He has done." This next step is one that proves to be challenging for many because it requires us to PRAISE God despite what we are going through. I have heard so many people ask how they can praise God when they are being tested. My question is, what is stopping you from praising God while you are going through? Regardless of the situation, God is still good, and He is still faithful. Our ability to praise during trials is an act of faith. You see, it is very easy to praise God when things are going great in life but rejoicing with a shout of "Lord I love you," "Hallelujah" or "God you're worthy" when all hell is breaking loose in life, shows true faith in God. It shows your trust in HIS will for your life.

As we PRAY and PRAISE, God promises to give us the "peace that surpasses all understanding to guard [our] hearts and minds in Christ Jesus" (Philippians 4: 7).

SLAY: You've prayed and praised, so now it's time to slay, but the crucial part of this phase is for you to take a step back and remove self out of the situation. I know you are wondering how you can slay if you take a step back. It is imperative for self to step back so that God can step up! If you could have overcome this alone, I'm quite sure you would have tried. If you're honest, you probably have tried. It's not about YOU and what YOU can do, but it's about what GOD can do through you. Think back to chapter 19, and remember that David didn't look to himself to slay the giant in front of him. Instead, he looked to God to deliver him from his enemy. In your storm, you job is to PRAY and PRAISE. Then step back and watch God SLAY the giants in your life.

REPEAT: While we would love to live on the mountaintop and bask in the beauty of the sun daily, the reality is that there will be valley moments. Storms will arise at any given moment, so we must be always be prepared. The final part of this concept is simple. No matter what you are facing, PRAY, PRAISE, SLAY, and REPEAT those steps as necessary.

I never thought life's journey would become so difficult or take me on such an emotional rollercoaster. There were times that I thought that I would never smile or truly enjoy life again, but God! He removed the heartache, bitterness, brokenness, and pain and replaced it with praise. Through those four words: PRAY, PRAISE, SLAY, and REPEAT, not only did God give me peace, he restored my joy. I was able to smile and embrace happiness in spite of my circumstances. God renewed my faith and gave me a new love for life.

Today, I pray that He would do the same for you.

NOTES
BASED ON THE READING, WHAT IS
GOD SAYING TO YOU?

_____

_____

_____

_____

_____

_____

_____

_____

_____

_____

_____

_____

_____

_____

_____

_____

_____

NOTES
BASED ON THE READING, WHAT IS
GOD SAYING TO YOU?

_____

_____

_____

_____

_____

_____

_____

_____

_____

_____

_____

_____

_____

_____

_____

_____

_____

_____

NOTES
BASED ON THE READING, WHAT IS
GOD SAYING TO YOU?

_____

_____

_____

_____

_____

_____

_____

_____

_____

_____

_____

_____

_____

_____

_____

_____

NOTES
BASED ON THE READING, WHAT IS GOD SAYING TO YOU?

_____

_____

_____

_____

_____

_____

_____

_____

_____

_____

_____

_____

_____

_____

_____

_____

_____

NOTES
BASED ON THE READING, WHAT IS
GOD SAYING TO YOU?

_____

_____

_____

_____

_____

_____

_____

_____

_____

_____

_____

_____

_____

_____

_____

_____

_____

NOTES
BASED ON THE READING, WHAT IS GOD SAYING TO YOU?

_____

_____

_____

_____

_____

_____

_____

_____

_____

_____

_____

_____

_____

_____

_____

_____

NOTES
BASED ON THE READING, WHAT IS
GOD SAYING TO YOU?

_____

_____

_____

_____

_____

_____

_____

_____

_____

_____

_____

_____

_____

_____

_____

_____

_____

Difficult roads often lead to beautiful destinations. The journey may be difficult, but do not give up. The best is yet to come!

Peace and Blessings,
Shae

ABOUT THE AUTHOR

Shae Sterling is a servant, mother, writer, speaker, educator, visionary, and owner of Next Level Faith Apparel (www.nextlevelfaithapparel.com). More importantly, she is a woman on fire for God! Shae is a servant leader dedicated to making a change in not only her community but the world. Shae has a powerful testimony of growing in faith while overcoming tragedy and brokenness. She now works to help others fight through their valley moments realizing that God will provide beauty for ashes. You can connect with Shae via the following platforms:
Facebook: www.facebook.com/shae.sterling.9
Instagram: @youniquelyshae